Fetch!

TERRIERS

Valerie Bodden

CREATIVE
PAPER BACKS

published by Creative Paperbacks
P.O. Box 227, Mankato, Minnesota 56002
Creative Paperbacks is an imprint of
The Creative Company
www.thecreativecompany.us

design and production by
Christine Vanderbeek
art direction by Rita Marshall
printed in the United States of America

photographs by Alamy (AF archive,
Adrian Sherratt), Dreamstime (Adam
Edwards, Erik Lam, Sergey Lavrentev,
Marlonneke, Steven Mcsweeny), Getty
Images (STAN HONDA/AFP), iStockphoto
(Eric Isselee, Dmitry Kalinovsky, Mikko
Pitkänen, rusm, Ben Smidt, Andrey Yakovlev),
Mary Evans Picture Library (Lyman Frank
Baum Illustration), Shutterstock (Alias Studiot
Oy, eAlisa, Maja H., Eric Isselee, Jagodka,
Erik Lam, metrjohn, Lipowski Milan,
Neveshkin Nikolay, Robynrg, Susan Schmitz,
Viorel Sima, SmileStudio, Nikolai Tsvetkov,
Vicente Barcelo Varona, violetblue,
WilleeCole)

library of congress
cataloging-in-publication data
Bodden, Valerie.
Terriers / Valerie Bodden.
p. cm. — (Fetch!)
SUMMARY: A brief overview of the physical
characteristics, personality traits, and habits
of the terrier breeds, as well as descriptions
of famous pop-culture terriers such as Toto.
Includes index.

ISBN 978-1-60818-365-4 (hardcover)
ISBN 978-0-89812-944-1 (pbk)
1. Terriers—Juvenile literature. I. Title.
SF429.T3B63 2014
636.755—dc23   2013005521

first edition
9 8 7 6 5 4 3 2 1

TABLE OF CONTENTS

ENERGETIC TERRIERS

Terriers are *breeds* of dogs. Terriers are strong and brave. They are smart and pushy, too. They have a lot of energy.

WHAT DO TERRIERS LOOK LIKE?

There are many breeds of terriers. Yorkshire (*YORK-shur*) terriers are some of the smallest terriers. They are only eight or nine inches (20–23 cm) tall. They weigh about as much as a newborn baby. Airedales (*AIR-dales*) are the biggest terriers. They are 23 inches (58 cm) tall and weigh about 55 pounds (25 kg).

Australian Terrier   *Bedlington Terrier*   *Border Terrier*   *Cairn Terrier*

Dandy Dinmont Terrier   *Irish Terrier*   *Jack Russell Terrier*   *Kerry Blue Terrier*

Manchester Terrier   *Miniature Schnauzer*   *Norfolk Terrier*   *Scottish Terrier*

Skye Terrier   *Staffordshire Bull Terrier*   *Welsh Schnauzer*   *Wire Fox Terrier*

Fetch!

Some terriers have **erect** ears. Others have ears that fold forward. Terriers can be white, black, light brown, or reddish. Or they can be more than one color. Most terriers have short fur.

The West Highland white terrier (below)
is one of many kinds of terriers.

· 9 ·

TERRIER PUPPIES

Newborn terrier puppies weigh less than one pound (0.5 kg). The fur of some breeds changes color as the puppy gets older. Kerry blue terriers are born with black fur. As they grow, the fur becomes bluish gray.

Terrier puppies stay close to each other

TERRIERS ON THE SCREEN

Terriers can be seen in many movies and TV shows. The TV show *Wishbone* was about a Jack Russell terrier who dressed in costumes to act out stories. Jock is a Scottish terrier in the Walt Disney movie *Lady and the Tramp*.

Jock the Scottish terrier (left) is shown with other dogs in Lady and the Tramp.

Fetch!

TERRIERS AND PEOPLE

People have used terriers to hunt for 500 years. Terriers hunt rats, foxes, and otters. Today, some kinds of terriers work as police dogs or *therapy dogs*. Some are *show dogs*.

A smooth fox terrier named Adam (right) won awards at the 2013 Westminster Kennel Club Dog Show.

Most terriers are good with kids. Some terriers can be too wild with very young children, though. Terrier puppies are sometimes hard to train. Adult terriers can be calmer. But they might have some bad habits. Both male and female terriers make good pets.

Terriers like to run and play but can be taught to fetch things like slippers.

WHAT DO TERRIERS LIKE TO DO?

Most terriers like to live indoors with their family. Terriers need exercise every day. Terriers should be brushed once or twice a week. Terriers with longer coats may need to get their fur clipped.

Longhaired terriers like the Cairn (right) need to have their fur trimmed regularly.

Fetch!

Terriers love to play with their owners. And they love to chase. Throw a ball for your terrier to fetch. You will both have lots of fun!

A FAMOUS TERRIER

The dog Toto from *The Wizard of Oz* is a Cairn terrier. Toto joins his owner Dorothy on her adventures in the Land of Oz. The dog that played Toto in the *Wizard of Oz* movie was a female. She made $125 a week for her work. She starred in 13 other movies as well. In some books about Oz, Toto can talk.

GLOSSARY

breeds kinds of an animal with certain traits, such as long ears or a good nose

erect standing upright

show dogs dogs that compete in dog shows, where judges decide which dogs are the best examples of each breed

therapy dogs dogs that help people who are sick or hurt by letting the people pet and enjoy them

READ MORE

Green, Sara. *Yorkshire Terriers*. Minneapolis: Bellwether Media, 2009.

————. *West Highland White Terriers*. Minneapolis: Bellwether Media, 2010.

Johnson, Jinny. *Yorkshire Terrier*. North Mankato, Minn.: Smart Apple Media, 2013.

WEBSITES

Bailey's Responsible Dog Owner's Coloring Book
http://classic.akc.org/pdfs/public_education/coloring_book.pdf
Print out pictures to color, and learn more about caring for a pet dog.

Just Dog Breeds: Border Terrier
http://www.www.justdogbreeds.com/border-terrier.html
Learn more about border terriers, and check out lots of terrier pictures.

Every effort has been made to ensure that these sites are suitable for children, that they have educational value, and that they contain no inappropriate material. However, because of the nature of the Internet, it is impossible to guarantee that these sites will remain active indefinitely or that their contents will not be altered.

INDEX